LIFEGUARD DOGS

by Natalie Lunis

Consultant: Commander Ferruccio Pilenga
Scuola Italiana Cani Salvataggio
(Italian School of Water Rescue Dogs)

New York, New York

Credits

Cover and Title Page, © SICS Scuola Italiana Cani Salvataggio; Cover TR, © SICS Scuola Italiana Cani Salvataggio; Cover CR, TIZIANA FABI/AFP/Getty Images; Cover BR, © REX USA/Colin Shepherd; TOC, © SICS Scuola Italiana Cani Salvataggio; 4, © finasteride/Getty; 5, © SICS Scuola Italiana Cani Salvataggio; 6, © Riccardo De Luca/Associated Press; 7, © Europics/Newscom; 8, © CB2/ZOB/WENN/Newscom; 9, © SICS Scuola Italiana Cani Salvataggio; 10–11, © SICS Scuola Italiana Cani Salvataggio; 12, © PhotoAlto/Alamy; 13T, © Mark Raycroft/Minden Pictures/Corbis; 13B, © Lynn M. Stone/KimballStock; 14T, © Adriano Bacchella/Naturepl.com; 14BR, © Daisy Images/Alamy; 15L, © Peter Llewellyn/Alamy; 15TR, © Dale Spartas/Corbis; 16, © SICS Scuola Italiana Cani Salvataggio; 17, © SICS Scuola Italiana Cani Salvataggio; 18, © AP Photo/Courtesy of Italian School of Canine Lifeguards; 19, © SICS Scuola Italiana Cani Salvataggio; 20, © TIZIANA FABI/AFP/Getty Images; 21, © SICS Scuola Italiana Cani Salvataggio; 22, © AP Photo/Courtesy of Italian School of Canine Lifeguards; 23, © SICS Scuola Italiana Cani Salvataggio; 24, © SICS Scuola Italiana Cani Salvataggio; 25T, © REX USA/Colin Shepherd; 25B, © Steve Jamieson; 26, © Phil Monckton; 27, © SICS Scuola Italiana Cani Salvataggio; 28, © TIZIANA FABI/AFP/Getty Images; 29T, © Eric Isselee/Shutterstock; 29C, © Ron Kimball/KimballStock; 29B, © Ron Kimball/KimballStock.

Publisher: Kenn Goin
Editorial Director: Adam Siegel
Creative Director: Spencer Brinker
Design: Dawn Beard Creative
Photo Researcher: Picture Perfect Professionals, LLC

Library of Congress Cataloging-in-Publication Data

Lunis, Natalie, author.
  Lifeguard dogs / by Natalie Lunis ; consultant, Commander Ferruccio Pilenga, Italian School of Water Rescue Dogs.
    pages cm. — (Dog heroes)
  Audience: Ages 7–12.
  Includes bibliographical references and index.
  ISBN 978-1-62724-088-8 (library binding) — ISBN 1-62724-088-8 (library binding)
  1. Pilenga, Ferruccio—Juvenile literature. 2. Scuola italiana cani salvataggio—Juvenile literature. 3. Water rescue dogs—Juvenile literature. 4. Working dogs—Juvenile literature. 5. Lifeguards—Juvenile literature. I. Pilenga, Ferruccio, consultant. II. Title. III. Series: Dog heroes.
  SF428.55.L86 2014
  636.73—dc23

                    2013037773

For more information, write to Bearport Publishing Company, Inc., 45 West 21st Street, Suite 3B, New York, New York 10010. Printed in the United States of America.

10 9 8 7 6 5 4 3 2 1

Table of Contents

Beach Rescue

On the morning of July 15, 2012, the weather at Sant'Agostino Beach in Italy was clear and calm—just perfect for a swim. Shortly before noon, however, the wind picked up. Soon, it blew so hard that it pushed two swimmers dangerously far from shore. One of them was an eight-year-old girl. The other was a 64-year-old man. Unable to make it back to the beach, the two swimmers were stranded in the choppy ocean water.

A view of the water near Sant'Agostino Beach

Fortunately, a lifeguard named Ariel was on duty. With her partner, she managed to swim out and safely bring both swimmers back. The two rescues added up to a good day's work for a pair of lifeguards, but most of the time such an event wouldn't make the headlines. This time it did. That's because one of the lifeguards—Ariel— was a dog.

Ariel

Sant'Agostino Beach is about 50 miles (80 km) from Rome, Italy's capital city.

A Special Gift

The fact that Ariel is a dog isn't the only reason her story made headlines. The yellow Labrador retriever had once belonged to a very famous person—Italian soccer star Francesco Totti. Francesco, who played for the team that represents Rome, had received Ariel when she was just a puppy. The little dog was a gift from one of the soccer team's **sponsors**.

Francesco Totti in action during a game in 2013

Francesco wanted to make a difference to people throughout his country. So he decided to **donate** Ariel to a very special organization—the Italian School of Water Rescue Dogs. Known in Italy as Scuola Italiana Cani Salvataggio, or SICS for short, this training center is **dedicated** to saving people's lives in a new and unusual way.

Francesco received another Labrador puppy at the same time as Ariel. That puppy, named Flipper, was also placed with the school.

Francesco Totti with Ariel

A New Kind of School

Today, SICS has fifteen training centers in different parts of Italy. More than 300 dogs and their **handlers** watch over beaches throughout the country. The lifeguard teams, known as K9 units, have rescued dozens of people.

During the 1980s, however, there was no lifeguard school for dogs. In fact, at that time there was only one human-and-dog water rescue team. It was made up of Ferruccio Pilenga, a **civil protection** worker, and his Newfoundland dog, Mas.

Ferruccio and Mas

To work as a team, a dog that is training at SICS and its handler must know and trust each other. For this reason, the dogs live with their human partners as part of their families.

Ferruccio and Mas worked side by side to find the best ways to help swimmers and boaters in trouble. After a while, they started training with the Italian **Coast Guard**. They were able to perform rescues with its members, using Coast Guard boats and other equipment. Then, in 1989, Ferruccio started SICS so that other people and their dogs could learn to perform the kinds of rescues he and Mas had developed.

Teams of lifeguard dogs and their handlers from the Italian School of Water Rescue Dogs

A Bold Dream

The idea of teaming up with dogs to perform water rescues had been forming in Ferruccio Pilenga's mind for a long time. While he was a civil protection worker, he had seen search-and-rescue dogs in action after earthquakes. The memory of the dogs' strength and courage stayed with him. Ferruccio also could not forget a **legend** he had heard about sailors who traveled the seas long ago.

Ferruccio and Mas at work

In the story, a large ship is hit by a storm. A huge wave crashes against the ship and washes one of the sailors overboard. Suddenly, a black shape leaps into the rough waters and pulls the drowning man back to the ship and to safety. According to the legend, the black shape was a Newfoundland dog—just like Mas. Ferruccio researched the history behind these dogs, including their heroic work on sailing ships. Today, thanks to Ferruccio, some SICS dogs continue this tradition by accompanying sailors on ships.

Newfoundland is a large island off the eastern coast of Canada. Newfoundland dogs are named after this island because it is where people first developed the **breed**.

The Top Breeds

According to the rules set by the Italian School of Water Rescue Dogs, any dog can train there to save lives. It must, however, be "**confident** in the water" and weigh at least 55 pounds (25 kg). This weight requirement is important, since a rescue dog needs to be more than just a good swimmer. It must also be strong enough to pull people and boats through the water.

Newfoundlands easily pass the weight test at the school. An adult of this breed can weigh up to 150 pounds (68 kg).

Not surprisingly, most of the dogs that have trained at the school are Newfoundlands, like Mas. The two other breeds that **excel** at water rescue are Labrador retrievers—like Ariel and Flipper—and golden retrievers.

Labrador retriever

Golden retriever

Strong Swimmers

What makes Newfoundlands such great lifeguard dogs? In addition to their size and strength, they have bodies that are built for swimming. A Newfoundland's large paws are **webbed**, like a duck's. The webbing, or extra skin, helps the dog push more water, which makes each **stroke** more powerful. A Newfoundland also has a muscular tail that acts like a **rudder**. The strong tail helps the dog steer itself as it moves through the ocean.

A Newfoundland swimming

A Newfoundland has a thick coat with two different layers of fur. The coat helps the dog stay warm and dry, even in icy cold water.

Labrador retrievers and golden retrievers are also powerful swimmers. Both of these dogs have strong muscles that allow them to move easily through the water. They both also have rudder-like tails that help them steer their bodies.

Golden retrievers (left) and Labrador retrievers (right) are not as furry as Newfoundlands, but, like Newfoundlands, they have waterproof coats.

Focused and Fearless

Newfoundlands and Labrador retrievers don't just have the right physical qualities to be lifeguard dogs. They are also able to pay attention to the water and spot problems right away. That's what happened when Ariel performed her very first rescue. At the time, a 23-year-old swimmer found herself in trouble in deep water. She started waving her arms for help. Ariel, who was in a raft with her handler, was the first to see the struggling woman.

Italian lifeguards and their canine partners sometimes keep an eye on swimmers from boats like this one.

Lifeguard dogs must also be fearless. Newfoundlands and Labrador retrievers are known for diving into the waves whenever they can. This **trait** comes in handy when it is time for them to start training to save lives.

To spring into action, a lifeguard dog might have to take off from a beach, a **pier**, a raft, a boat, or even a helicopter that is hovering above the water.

Starting Out at School

Dogs can start training at the Italian School of Water Rescue Dogs when they are puppies or adults. However, instructors believe that the best age to start is at about four months. Whether the new "students" are puppies or adults, their first lessons focus on **obedience**. The dogs work on paying attention to their handlers and getting along well with other dogs.

Dogs of different ages, from puppies to adults, learn the beginning steps of water rescue together.

For the next set of lessons, the dogs learn to feel comfortable in the water. Then they learn to swim alongside their handlers. During this time, a dog and its handler are practicing more than just swimming skills, however. They are building the sense of trust and teamwork that they will need in order to perform rescues together.

In the beginning, instructors and handlers make the water training seem like play for the dogs. They believe that the dogs will learn better if they start out by enjoying the time they spend in the water.

More to Learn

In more advanced courses at the school, dogs become familiar with special equipment, such as a **harness**. They also try out different types of life-saving actions. For example, during a rescue, a dog and its handler might need to jump from a boat or raft. The dogs learn to follow their human partners into the water without losing any precious time.

Usually, it takes two to three years of training for a dog and its handler to gain the skills they need to become a life-saving team. Here, a dog and its trainer practice diving into the water together.

Once in the water, a dog might swim side-by-side with its handler to reach the victim. The dog can then **tow** the victim—who holds onto the dog's harness—back to safety. Or, the dog might tow its handler to the victim. This helps the handler save his or her strength in order to be able to give the victim **CPR** while still in the water. Sometimes, saving a few minutes by not waiting to give CPR until the victim is back on land can mean the difference between life and death.

Dogs and their handlers must pass a series of tests before they can do rescue work on Italy's beaches.

This woman holds onto the dog's harness as the lifeguard dog swims back to shore.

The Toughest Rescues

After the dogs at the school are trained and pass their tests, some of them prepare for the most daring and difficult rescues of all. Together with their handlers, they learn how to jump into the ocean from high above the water—either from the **decks** of large Coast Guard rescue boats or from helicopters. They train for these kinds of rescues in order to get to victims who would be hard or impossible to reach from shore.

A helicopter hovers three to six feet (1 to 2 m) above the water while a dog and its handler jump out.

How does the K9 unit get back on the boat or helicopter with the victims they have saved? In both cases, they need help from the crew on board. This is especially true during a **heli-rescue**, which ends with the aircrew using a **winch** to help lift those in the water to safety.

A dog and its handler being raised back onto a helicopter

Banned from the Beach

Besides Italy, a few other countries in Europe rely on lifeguard dogs to help carry out water rescues. Most of the time, the dogs accompany their human handlers on fast-paced missions. In Italy, the rescue teams use boats or helicopters to reach people who need help right away. Sometimes, however, especially in Italy, the dogs **patrol** the beaches with human lifeguards. The teams watch and listen for the first signs of trouble.

Lifeguard dogs in Italy patrolling a beach with their human handlers

In England, one dog became famous for patrolling the beach. Bilbo, a Newfoundland, was trained by his owner, lifeguard Steve Jamieson. In 2007, the lifeguard dog made headlines when he saved a swimmer. Then in 2008, something truly shocking happened. **Officials** decided that Bilbo had to leave because no dogs were allowed on the beach!

Bilbo and his handler, Steve

Bilbo to the rescue

Bilbo has won praise for helping to rescue three people while working as a lifeguard dog.

The Next Wave?

People were upset when Bilbo was **banned** from the beach. A number of **petitions**, with thousands of signatures on each one, were sent to the officials in charge. Fortunately, as a result of the strong feelings people expressed, Bilbo was allowed back. Together with Steve, he was able to visit the beach twice a week to help teach people about water safety.

Steve and Bilbo also visit schools to spread their message about staying safe at the beach.

In Italy, lifeguard dogs are also very popular with beachgoers. As a result of the dogs' success, perhaps more countries will recognize the special talents of these furry, four-legged lifeguards. Once that happens, dogs will not only be allowed on the beach—they will be welcome there!

Lifeguard dogs taking a break

Like Bilbo, some of Italy's lifeguard dogs have teamed up with their human partners to teach beachgoers about safe ways to swim and enjoy the water.

27

Just the Facts

- After a lifeguard dog in Italy passes the test that allows it to perform rescues, it receives a certificate. To continue working on beaches and in the water, it must take the test again once every year.

- In 1815, Napoleon Bonaparte (1769–1821), the former emperor of France, fell off a boat and was saved from drowning by a Newfoundland dog.

- A Newfoundland's two-layer coat stays waterproof even during a long swim. In fact, if someone lifts the top layer after the swim, the bottom layer will be completely dry.

- One Newfoundland can pull a boat holding 20 people.

- When K9 units practice water rescues in Italy, instructors from the school play the role of drowning victims.

Common Breeds: LIFEGUARD DOGS

Newfoundland

Golden retriever

Labrador retriever

banned (BAND) not allowed

breed (BREED) a kind of dog

civil protection (SIV-il pruh-TEK-shuhn) a government department in Italy that helps people in emergencies

Coast Guard (KOHST GARD) a branch of the military that protects a nation's coasts and comes to the aid of boats and ships in trouble

confident (KON-fuh-duhnt) comfortable with doing something

CPR (see-pee-AR) letters standing for cardiopulmonary resuscitation; a type of rescue where a person blows air into the mouth and then presses down on the chest of someone whose heart has stopped

decks (DEKS) the upper levels of boats

dedicated (DED-uh-*kayt*-id) working for a particular task or purpose

donate (DOH-nayt) to give something as a gift

excel (ek-SELL) to perform very well

handlers (HAND-lurz) people who train and work with dogs

harness (HAR-niss) a device attached to an animal that allows people to hold on to it

heli-rescue (HEL-i-*res*-kyoo) a shortened way of saying "helicopter rescue"

legend (LEJ-uhnd) a story from long ago that is often based on some facts but cannot be proven true

obedience (oh-BEE-dee-uhnss) following a handler's commands, such as "sit" and "stay"

officials (uh-FISH-uhlz) people who hold offices or important positions

patrol (puh-TROHL) to walk around an area to protect it

petitions (puh-TISH-uhnz) written requests

pier (PEER) a structure built over water that is used as a walkway or a landing place for boats

rudder (RUHD-ur) a movable flat piece of wood or metal that is attached to the back of a boat and is used for steering

sponsors (SPON-surz) companies that support a team

stroke (STROHK) a set of movements that is repeated over and over in swimming

tow (TOH) to pull something

trait (TRAYT) a quality or characteristic of a person or an animal

webbed (WEBD) having toes connected by skin

winch (WINCH) a machine that uses rope or cable to pull or raise something

Bibliography

Israely, Jeff. "Canine Lifeguards Hit Italy's Beaches." *Time.* August 20, 2009. (http://content.time.com/time/world/article/0,8599,1917618,00.html)

Italian School of Water Rescue Dogs (www.waterrescuedogs.com/)

Weisbord, Merrily, and Kim Kachanoff. *Dogs with Jobs: Working Dogs Around the World.* New York: Pocket Books (2000).

Read More

Oldfield, Dawn Bluemel. *Newfoundland: Water Rescuer (Big Dogs Rule).* New York: Bearport (2012).

Osborne, Mary Pope, and Natalie Pope Boyce. *Dog Heroes (Magic Tree House Fact Tracker).* New York: Random House (2011).

Rudolph, Jessica. *Labrador Retriever: Most Popular (Big Dogs Rule).* New York: Bearport (2012).

Ruffin, Frances E. *Water Rescue Dogs (Dog Heroes).* New York: Bearport (2006).

Learn More Online

Visit these Web sites to learn more about lifeguard dogs:

www.akc.org/breeds/golden_retriever/index.cfm

www.akc.org/breeds/labrador_retriever/index.cfm

www.akc.org/breeds/newfoundland/index.cfm

www.bilbosays.com/

About the Author

Natalie Lunis has written over fifty nonfiction books for children. She lives in New York's lower Hudson River Valley.